# BEST mum EVER

TIM FENTON

summersdale

BEST MUM EVER

First published as *Bestest Mum Ever* in 2011

This updated edition copyright © Summersdale Publishers Ltd, 2016

Illustrations © Shutterstock

Summersdale Publishers Ltd
46 West Street
Chichester
West Sussex
PO19 1RP
UK

www.summersdale.com

Printed and bound in China

ISBN: 978-1-84953-810-7

Substantial discounts on bulk quantities of Summersdale books are available to corporations, professional associations and other organisations. For details contact Nicky Douglas by telephone: +44 (0) 1243 756902, fax: +44 (0) 1243 786300 or email: nicky@summersdale.com.

TO.......................................................

FROM...................................................

A MOTHER'S
LOVE FOR HER CHILD
IS LIKE NOTHING ELSE
IN THE WORLD.

Agatha Christie

IF EVOLUTION REALLY WORKS, HOW COME MOTHERS ONLY HAVE TWO HANDS?

Milton Berle

A MOTHER
UNDERSTANDS WHAT
A CHILD DOES
NOT SAY.

Jewish proverb

ANY **MOTHER** COULD PERFORM THE JOBS OF SEVERAL AIR TRAFFIC **CONTROLLERS** WITH EASE.

Lisa Alther

THINGS THAT MUMS CAN DO WITH ONE HAND TIED BEHIND THEIR BACK:

Organise the week ahead for the entire family - pets included!

Know when their
children are up
to no good

Pull Formula One-style
car manoeuvres when
parking the car at a
supermarket

Juggle a houseful of children or a roomful of employees with ease

Create a culinary showstopper for every special occasion

Play a mean game
of Scrabble

Make it all
better

Get the old family photo albums out and open to the baby pictures before your visitors have even sat down

A MOTHER IS ONE
TO WHOM YOU HURRY
WHEN YOU ARE
TROUBLED.

Emily Dickinson

THERE IS NO WAY
TO BE A **PERFECT**
MOTHER, AND A MILLION
WAYS TO BE A
**GOOD ONE.**

Jill Churchill

A MOTHER'S HEART
IS A PATCHWORK
OF LOVE.

Anonymous

MOTHER IS THE
ONE WE COUNT ON
FOR THE THINGS THAT
MATTER MOST OF ALL.

Katharine Butler
Hathaway

MY MOTHER IS A
WALKING MIRACLE.

Leonardo DiCaprio

IF YOU HAVE A MOM,
THERE IS NOWHERE
YOU ARE LIKELY TO GO
WHERE A PRAYER
HAS NOT ALREADY BEEN.

Robert Brault

THE ART OF
MOTHERING IS TO
TEACH THE ART OF
LIVING TO CHILDREN.

Elaine Heffner

IF MEN HAD TO
HAVE BABIES, THEY
WOULD ONLY EVER
HAVE ONE EACH.

Diana, Princess of Wales

A WOMAN IS LIKE A
**TEABAG.**
YOU CAN'T TELL HOW
STRONG SHE IS UNTIL
YOU PUT HER IN
**HOT WATER.**

Anonymous

WHERE THERE IS A
MOTHER IN THE HOME,
MATTERS GO WELL.

Amos Bronson Alcott

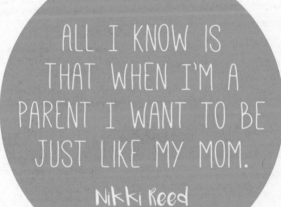

ALL I KNOW IS
THAT WHEN I'M A
PARENT I WANT TO BE
JUST LIKE MY MOM.

Nikki Reed

IF LOVE IS SWEET
AS A FLOWER,
THEN MY MOTHER
IS THAT SWEET
FLOWER OF LOVE.

Stevie Wonder

THE NATURAL STATE
OF MOTHERHOOD IS
UNSELFISHNESS.

Jessica Lange

# YOU KNOW YOU'RE A MUM WHEN...

... you count the number of chips on each child's plate to keep the peace at mealtimes.

... your dream date is
Fireman Sam.

... you realise you
now sound like your
own mother.

... you can rustle up a feast to rival Nigella from leftovers in the fridge.

... you accidentally take your childs PE kit to the gym.

... you automatically ignore all white clothes in the shops – you don't do white any more!

... you find yourself telling anyone who'll listen just what a genius your child is.

... you can't open the
fridge door due
to the amount of
childrens artwork
stuck to it.

WHEN A CHILD
NEEDS A MOTHER
TO TALK TO, NOBODY
ELSE BUT A MOTHER
WILL DO.

Erica Jong

A MOTHER'S HAPPINESS
IS LIKE A BEACON,
**LIGHTING UP**
THE FUTURE BUT
REFLECTED ALSO ON THE
PAST IN THE GUISE OF
**FOND MEMORIES.**

Honoré de Balzac

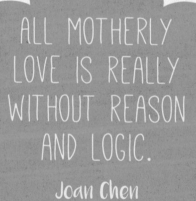

ALL MOTHERLY
LOVE IS REALLY
WITHOUT REASON
AND LOGIC.

Joan Chen

FOR MOST EXHAUSTED MUMS, THEIR IDEA OF 'WORKING OUT' IS A GOOD, ENERGETIC LIE-DOWN.

Kathy Lette

BEAUTIFUL AS
WAS MAMMA'S
FACE, IT BECAME
**INCOMPARABLY**
MORE LOVELY WHEN
SHE SMILED, AND
SEEMED TO **ENLIVEN**
EVERYTHING ABOUT HER.

Leo Tolstoy

AN OUNCE OF MOTHER
IS WORTH A TON
OF PRIEST.

Spanish proverb

MY MOTHER MADE A
**BRILLIANT**
IMPRESSION UPON MY
CHILDHOOD LIFE. SHE
SHONE FOR ME LIKE THE
**EVENING STAR.**

Winston Churchill

THERE IS NO VELVET
SO SOFT AS A
MOTHER'S LAP,
NO ROSE SO LOVELY AS
HER SMILE, NO PATH
SO FLOWERY AS THAT
IMPRINTED WITH HER
FOOTSTEPS.

Edward Thomson

TO DESCRIBE MY MOTHER WOULD BE TO WRITE ABOUT A HURRICANE IN ITS PERFECT POWER.

Maya Angelou

I SHALL
NEVER FORGET
MY MOTHER, FOR IT
WAS SHE WHO PLANTED
AND **NURTURED** THE
FIRST SEEDS OF GOOD
WITHIN ME.

Immanuel Kant

WHEN YOU ARE A
MOTHER, YOU ARE
NEVER REALLY ALONE
IN YOUR THOUGHTS.

Sophia Loren

MAKING THE DECISION
TO HAVE A CHILD IS...
FOREVER TO HAVE

# YOUR HEART

GO WALKING AROUND
OUTSIDE YOUR BODY.

## Elizabeth Stone

A MOTHER'S ARMS ARE
MADE OF TENDERNESS
AND CHILDREN SLEEP
SOUNDLY IN THEM.

Victor Hugo

# THINGS THAT MAKE MUMS CRY:

First burp, first word, first steps – first anything, really!

Seeing their child
off on the first day
of school

Watching their
future Oscar winner
in the school play

A home-made card
or painting to go
straight up on the
kitchen noticeboard

Reading a school
report - whatever
its content

Getting breakfast in bed on Mother's Day – who cares if the toast is cold?

When someone else does the washing up for a change

Seeing their scruffy
teenager all
smartened up for
the school dance

Weddings – it
doesn't matter who's
getting married!

SWEATER, N.:
GARMENT WORN BY
CHILD WHEN ITS MOTHER
IS FEELING CHILLY.

Ambrose Bierce

A MOTHER'S LOVE
PERCEIVES NO
IMPOSSIBILITIES.

Cornelia Paddock

UNTIL I GOT **MARRIED,** WHEN I USED TO GO OUT, MY MOTHER SAID GOODBYE TO ME AS THOUGH I WAS **EMIGRATING.**

Thora Hird

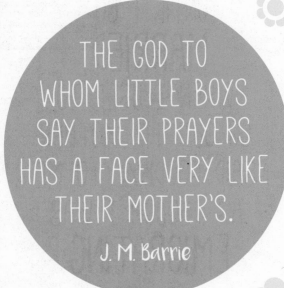

THE GOD TO
WHOM LITTLE BOYS
SAY THEIR PRAYERS
HAS A FACE VERY LIKE
THEIR MOTHER'S.

J. M. Barrie

A MOTHER'S
ARMS ARE MORE
COMFORTING THAN
ANYONE ELSE'S.

Diana, Princess of Wales

WHO RAN TO HELP ME
WHEN I FELL,
AND WOULD SOME
PRETTY STORY TELL,
OR KISS THE PLACE TO
MAKE IT WELL?
MY MOTHER.

**Ann Taylor**

MOTHER'S LOVE
IS BLISS, IS PEACE,
IT NEED NOT BE
ACQUIRED, IT NEED
NOT BE DESERVED.

Erich Fromm

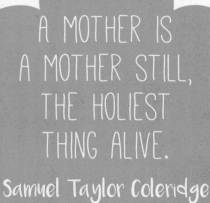

A MOTHER IS
A MOTHER STILL,
THE HOLIEST
THING ALIVE.

Samuel Taylor Coleridge

SHE WOULD
HAVE DESPISED THE
MODERN IDEA
OF WOMEN BEING EQUAL
TO MEN. EQUAL, INDEED!
SHE KNEW THEY WERE
SUPERIOR.

Elizabeth Gaskell

MY MOTHER HAD
A GREAT DEAL OF
**TROUBLE**
WITH ME, BUT I THINK
SHE **ENJOYED** IT.

Mark Twain

I CANNOT TELL HOW MUCH I OWE TO THE SOLEMN WORDS OF MY GOOD MOTHER.

Charles Spurgeon

MOTHER IS FAR
TOO CLEVER
TO UNDERSTAND
ANYTHING SHE
DOES NOT LIKE.

Arnold Bennett

A MOTHER'S HEART
IS THE CHILD'S
CLASSROOM.

Henry Ward Beecher

THINGS THAT ONLY
A MUM CAN TEACH:

Religion – 'You'd
better pray that
comes out in
the wash...'

Medical science –
'Don't cut off
your nose to spite
your face.'

Logic – 'Because I
said so.'

Mathematics – 'I'm going to give you until the count of three: one... two...'

Probability – 'You're going to be late for school if you don't leave now.'

Recycling – 'I'll have your guts for garters if you don't behave!'

Performance art – 'I feel like I'm talking to a brick wall.'

WHAT DO GIRLS DO
WHO HAVEN'T
ANY MOTHERS TO HELP
THEM THROUGH THEIR
TROUBLES?

Louisa May Alcott

A MOTHER HOLDS
HER CHILDREN'S HANDS
FOR A WHILE, THEIR
HEARTS FOREVER.

Anonymous

CHILDREN ARE A
GREAT COMFORT
IN YOUR OLD AGE — AND
THEY HELP YOU REACH
IT FASTER, TOO.

Lionel Kauffman

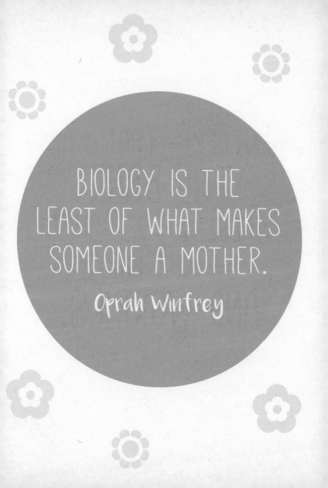

MOTHER — THAT WAS
THE BANK
WHERE WE DEPOSITED
ALL OUR HURTS
AND WORRIES.

Thomas De Witt Talmage

THE PATIENCE OF
A MOTHER MIGHT BE
LIKENED TO A TUBE OF
TOOTHPASTE — IT'S NEVER
QUITE ALL GONE.

Anonymous

MY MOTHER'S
WONDERFUL. TO ME,
SHE'S PERFECTION.
Michael Jackson

NO ONE KNOWS
LIKE A WOMAN
HOW TO SAY THINGS
THAT ARE AT ONCE
GENTLE AND DEEP.

Victor Hugo

SHE WAS OF THE
STUFF OF WHICH GREAT
MEN'S MOTHERS ARE
MADE. SHE WAS...
HATED AT TEA PARTIES,
FEARED IN SHOPS, AND
LOVED AT CRISES.

Thomas Hardy

NO INFLUENCE IS SO POWERFUL AS THAT OF THE MOTHER.

Sarah Josepha Hale

IT SEEMS TO ME THAT MY MOTHER WAS THE MOST SPLENDID WOMAN I EVER KNEW.

Charlie Chaplin

YOUTH FADES;
LOVE DROOPS;
THE LEAVES OF
FRIENDSHIP FALL;
A MOTHER'S SECRET
HOPE OUTLIVES
THEM ALL.

Oliver Wendell Holmes

A SMART MOTHER
MAKES OFTEN A BETTER
DIAGNOSIS THAN
A POOR DOCTOR.

August Bier

MY MOTHER'S GREAT...
SHE COULD STOP YOU
FROM DOING ANYTHING,
THROUGH A CLOSED
DOOR EVEN, WITH A
SINGLE LOOK.

Whoopi Goldberg

SECRET SKILLS
THAT ONLY MUMS
KNOW:

How to make a meal
that looks like a
smiley face

How to interpret squiggly drawings: 'What a lovely house! Oh, it's a dog – how beautiful!'

How to speak Baby

How to get everyone washed, dressed and out of the house before 9 a.m.

How to make a box into a robot/car/ spaceship

How to mend toys,
clothes and broken
hearts

How to frighten off
the monsters under
the bed

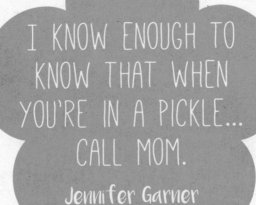

I KNOW ENOUGH TO KNOW THAT WHEN YOU'RE IN A PICKLE... CALL MOM.

Jennifer Garner

TO A CHILD'S EAR,
'MOTHER'
IS MAGIC IN ANY
LANGUAGE.

Arlene Benedict

HEAVEN IS AT THE
FEET OF MOTHERS.

Arabic proverb

I WILL ACCEPT LOTS
OF THINGS,
**BUT NOT WHEN**
SOMEONE INSULTS MY
MUM, THE
**NICEST PERSON**
IN THE WORLD.

Andy Murray

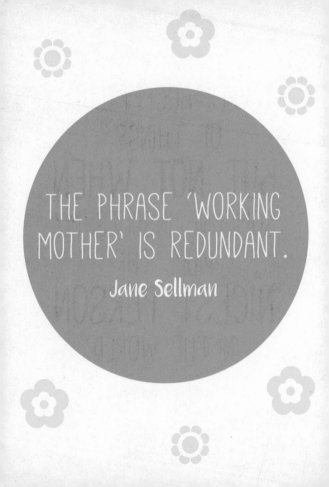

THE PHRASE 'WORKING MOTHER' IS REDUNDANT.

Jane Sellman

THE ONLY MOTHERS
IT IS SAFE TO FORGET
ON MOTHER'S DAY ARE
THE GOOD ONES.

Mignon McLaughlin

RAISING KIDS IS
PART JOY AND PART
GUERRILLA WARFARE.

Ed Asner

SHE NEVER QUITE
LEAVES HER CHILDREN
AT HOME,
EVEN WHEN SHE
DOESN'T TAKE
THEM ALONG.

Margaret Culkin Banning

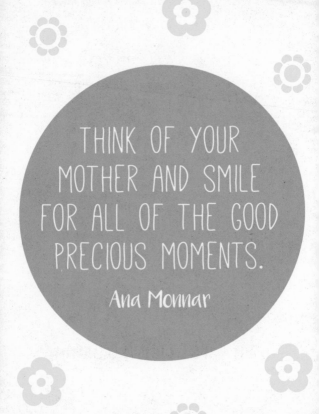

THINK OF YOUR
MOTHER AND SMILE
FOR ALL OF THE GOOD
PRECIOUS MOMENTS.

Ana Monnar

THERE IS ONLY ONE
PRETTY CHILD
IN THE WORLD, AND
EVERY MOTHER
HAS IT.

Chinese proverb

THE MOST BEAUTIFUL
WORD ON THE LIPS
OF MANKIND IS THE
WORD 'MOTHER'.

Kahlil Gibran

A MAN'S GOT TO DO
WHAT A MAN'S GOT TO
DO. A WOMAN MUST DO
WHAT HE CAN'T.

Rhonda Hansome

MOTHERS
ALWAYS KNOW.

Oprah Winfrey

MOTHERHOOD IS
NOT FOR THE
**FAINT-HEARTED.**
FROGS, SKINNED KNEES
AND THE INSULTS
OF TEENAGE GIRLS ARE
NOT MEANT FOR
**THE WIMPY.**

Danielle Steel

# AWARDS FOR THE BEST MUM EVER:

Bravery in the Face of Yucky Things

Culinary Genius

Royal Order of
Organisational
Prowess

# Extraordinary Alertness After a Night of No Sleep

## Queen of Solutions

Most Patient Parent

Kindest Nurse

Best Hand-holder

The Golden Car
Key Award for
Chauffeuring

# Most Attentive Listener

# Cheerleader in Chief

MOTHERS... WHO CARRY THE KEY OF OUR SOULS IN THEIR BOSOMS.

Oliver Wendell Holmes

SING OUT LOUD
IN THE CAR EVEN,
OR ESPECIALLY,
IF IT EMBARRASSES
YOUR CHILDREN.

Marilyn Penland

THE STRENGTH OF
MOTHERHOOD IS
GREATER THAN
NATURAL LAWS.

Barbara Kingsolver

NO PAINTER'S BRUSH
NOR POET'S PEN,
IN JUSTICE TO HER
FAME, HAS EVER
REACHED HALF
HIGH ENOUGH
TO WRITE A
MOTHER'S NAME.

*Anonymous*

CHILDREN KEEP US IN
CHECK. THEIR LAUGHTER
PREVENTS OUR HEARTS
FROM HARDENING.

Queen Rania of Jordan

SOME ARE KISSING
MOTHERS AND SOME
ARE SCOLDING MOTHERS,
BUT... MOST MOTHERS
KISS AND SCOLD
TOGETHER.

Pearl S. Buck

WHEN YOU LOOK AT
YOUR MOTHER,
YOU ARE LOOKING AT THE
PUREST LOVE
YOU WILL EVER KNOW.

Mitch Albom

CHILD-REARING MYTH #1: LABOUR ENDS WHEN THE BABY IS BORN.

Anonymous

BEFORE I GOT MARRIED, I HAD SIX THEORIES ABOUT **BRINGING UP** CHILDREN; NOW, I HAVE SIX CHILDREN AND **NO THEORIES.**

John Wilmot,
2nd Earl of Rochester

WOMEN, YOU KNOW, DO SELDOM FAIL TO MAKE THE STOUTEST MEN TURN TAIL.

Samuel Butler

A MOTHER IS SHE WHO
CAN TAKE THE PLACE OF
**ALL OTHERS**
BUT WHOSE PLACE NO
ONE ELSE CAN TAKE.

Gaspard Mermillod

THERE ARE ONLY TWO
THINGS A CHILD WILL
**SHARE WILLINGLY:**
COMMUNICABLE DISEASES
AND HIS MOTHER'S AGE.

Benjamin Spock

# THINGS IN
# MUM'S HANDBAG:

## Hand wipes

Spare pair of socks

Factor 50 sun cream

A seemingly endless
supply of tissues
and plasters

Emergency
chocolate supplies

Safety pins

Digital camera

Hairclips

Mittens on a string

Foldable anorak

A notebook and lots
of pens and pencils

MOTHER IS THE
ONE WE COUNT ON
FOR THE THINGS THAT
MATTER MOST OF ALL.

Katharine Butler
Hathaway

MOTHERHOOD IN ALL
ITS GUISES
AND PERMUTATIONS
IS MORE ART
THAN SCIENCE.

Melinda M. Marshall

GOD COULD NOT BE EVERYWHERE, SO HE CREATED MOTHERS.

Jewish proverb

WE HAVE CHARTS,
MAPS AND LISTS ON
THE FRIDGE,
ALL OVER THE HOUSE.
I SOMETIMES FEEL LIKE
I'M WITH THE CIA.

Kate Winslet

I THINK MY LIFE
BEGAN WITH WAKING
UP AND LOVING MY
MOTHER'S FACE.

George Eliot

A MOTHER IS NOT A
PERSON TO LEAN ON,
BUT A PERSON
TO MAKE LEANING
UNNECESSARY.

Dorothy Canfield Fisher

CHILDREN AND
MOTHERS NEVER TRULY
PART — BOUND IN THE
BEATING OF EACH
OTHER'S HEART.

Charlotte Gray

WORKING MOTHERS ARE
GUINEA PIGS
IN A SCIENTIFIC
EXPERIMENT TO SHOW
THAT SLEEP IS
NOT NECESSARY
TO HUMAN LIFE.

Anonymous

A SUBURBAN
MOTHER'S ROLE IS
TO DELIVER CHILDREN
OBSTETRICALLY
ONCE, AND BY CAR
FOR EVER AFTER.

Peter De Vries

THERE'S NOTHING LIKE
A MAMA-HUG.

Terri Guillemets

# NO LANGUAGE
## CAN EXPRESS THE POWER
## AND BEAUTY AND HEROISM
## AND MAJESTY OF A
# MOTHER'S LOVE.

### Edwin Hubbell Chapin

SHE MAY SCOLD
YOU FOR LITTLE
THINGS, BUT NEVER
FOR THE BIG ONES.

Harry S. Truman

YOU NEVER
GET REALLY
CROSS WITH ME,
EVEN WHEN...

... I come home
covered in mud from
head to toe.

... I leave my wet towel in a heap on the bathroom floor.

... I use your designer wardrobe as my dressing-up box.

... I drink milk straight from the carton.

... I wake you up complaining of nightmares before demanding a space in the bed.

... I never remember to turn the lights off when leaving a room.

... I forget that it's my turn to empty the dishwasher.

MOTHER IS THE
NAME FOR GOD IN THE
LIPS AND HEARTS OF
LITTLE CHILDREN.

William Makepeace
Thackeray

A FATHER'S GOODNESS
IS HIGHER THAN
THE MOUNTAIN;
A MOTHER'S GOODNESS
IS DEEPER THAN
THE SEA.

Japanese proverb

ONLY MOTHERS
CAN THINK OF THE
FUTURE — BECAUSE THEY
GIVE BIRTH TO IT IN
THEIR CHILDREN.

Maxim Gorky

WHATEVER ELSE IS
UNSURE IN THIS... WORLD
A MOTHER'S LOVE
IS NOT.

James Joyce

PARENTHOOD:
THE STATE OF BEING
BETTER CHAPERONED
THAN YOU WERE
BEFORE MARRIAGE.

Marcelene Cox

YOU WILL ALWAYS
BE YOUR CHILD'S
FAVOURITE TOY.

Vicki Lansky

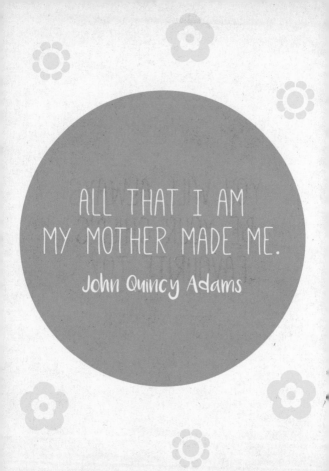

ALL THAT I AM
MY MOTHER MADE ME.

John Quincy Adams

THE HEART OF A
MOTHER IS A DEEP
ABYSS AT THE
BOTTOM OF WHICH
YOU WILL ALWAYS FIND
FORGIVENESS.

Honoré de Balzac

I COULDN'T LIVE
WITHOUT MY MUSIC,
MAN. OR ME MUM.

Robbie Williams

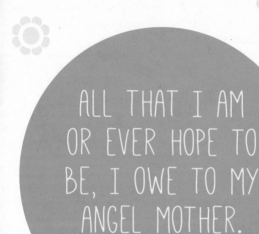

ALL THAT I AM
OR EVER HOPE TO
BE, I OWE TO MY
ANGEL MOTHER.

Abraham Lincoln

THE HAND THAT
ROCKS THE CRADLE
USUALLY IS ATTACHED
TO SOMEONE WHO
ISN'T GETTING
ENOUGH SLEEP.

John Fiebig

MOTHER IS THE
HEARTBEAT IN THE
HOME; AND WITHOUT
HER, THERE SEEMS TO
BE NO HEART THROB.

Leroy Brownlow

A MOTHER IS
THE TRUEST FRIEND
WE HAVE.

Washington Irving

I THOUGHT MY MOM'S
WHOLE PURPOSE
WAS TO BE MY MOM.
THAT'S HOW SHE
MADE ME FEEL.

Natasha Gregson Wagner

THERE WAS NEVER A
GREAT MAN WHO HAD
NOT A GREAT MOTHER
— IT IS HARDLY AN
EXAGGERATION.

Olive Schreiner

A LITTLE GIRL, ASKED
WHERE HER HOME
WAS, REPLIED, 'WHERE
MOTHER IS.'

Keith L. Brooks

# YOU'RE THE BEST MUM BECAUSE...

... you take me shopping until I've found exactly the right thing to wear.

... you always tell me
I can do it.

... you listen to all my
stories – and you
remember them.

... you know just how to cheer me up.

... you're my favourite person to natter with over a cup of tea.

... you always have time to talk.

... you know how to get red wine stains out of my best party outfit.

... you've never
resigned, despite
having lots of
reasons to!

... you're always
there for me.

THANK YOU
FOR BEING...

The best
mum ever!

If you're interested in finding out more about our books, find us on Facebook at **Summersdale Publishers** and follow us on Twitter at @Summersdale.

www.summersdale.com